I0483538

Business Secrets Every Small Business
Owner MUST Know To Succeed!

EXPLODE
YOUR SERIVCE
BUSINESS

FOR PENNIES

ROBERT BRUNELLE

EXPLODE YOUR SERVICE BUSINESS FOR PENNIES

by *Robert Brunelle*

All Rights Reserved. No part of this publication may be reproduced in any form or by any means, including scanning, photocopying, or otherwise without prior written permission of the copyright holder. Copyright © 2015

Table of Contents

Introduction

Increase Customer Retention

Hello and thank you for investing in this book. My name is Bob Brunelle. I started my first business in 1978 with a phone and a dream. No matter how much technology changes people still love great service and that's something that will never change. The marketing technique you will learn is from 30 years of me being in the carpet cleaning business. You can't find anything like this program on the Internet; I've searched and searched and searched and found nothing. The marketing technique I will share with you is so simple it will take very little effort to integrate with your business.

The great thing about this marketing strategy is it works with any service business.

1. Carpet cleaners.
2. Air conditioner repair.
3. Garage door repair.
4. Pest control.
5. Pool service.
5. Landscapers.

That's right, any service business that requires a repeat service call. I did it for over 30 years and it worked for me.

In the last 30 years I've owned 3 businesses in 3 states and I can assure you if you own a service business it this technique will work for you. I've spent thousands and thousands of dollars on programs that didn't work or would cost me too much money to implement. Some programs I bought I never even opened the package. If you're like me you know what happened, you bought a program and it sat on your bookshelf collecting dust and that's another $300 or $500 down the drain.

Most marketing programs never get down to the nuts and bolts of how the program works. They only talk about results but they never talk specifics; I mean like 1 2 3. When it comes to marketing time is your enemy.

You'll see as you go through my program that this book is nothing like that. As a small business person myself I know that implementing a marketing program has to be simple to implement and must function with your daily schedule. Most importantly, it must be cost effective. If you have a phone, a computer and a filing system this will work for you. The only thing it will cost you is time and if you're not as busy as you want to be that's one thing you should have plenty of.

Let me tell you what I don't want you to do, DO NOT changed this system. I can't stress this point enough. The reason I am stressing this point is that every company I sold that changed my system struggled or went out of business.

This book is not going to be 100 pages long. You have more important things to do like run your business. I will provide you with simple scripts to get you started right away. I am always available to customize scripts for your business. My email address is bob@,marketingforservicesbusiness.com feel free to contact me.

Let's get started making You money today!

1. What You Will Need

What you will need to get started

I told you that this is a very simple process. Let me show you how simple it is.

1. First thing you'll need is a phone; I know you have one of those.
2. You will need a filing system.
3. You will need a computer.

We mainly use the computer for a packaging system.

Now you're ready to get started. This will be one of the most inexpensive marketing programs you've ever purchased.

Remember my rule of thumb keep it simple. I don't know how much simpler it can be than this.

Okay, I'm excited let's go to the next chapter!

2. Packaging Your Services

Packaging Your Services

We are going to spend a good amount of time on this chapter. This is the backbone of the system. Once again this system should only be used in the order I have set up.

Why package your services? I'm glad you asked. What is the first thing a fast food restaurant asked you after you give them your order? "Would you like a small, medium or large?" Do I need to say anything more? These guys know how to make money. When it comes to packaging 3 packages is the magic number. Don't try reinventing the wheel it only confuses your customers.

If packages work for the fast food industry then why won't it work for service businesses? The good news is, it does work.

Let me tell you my story. Before I started packaging my services my average ticket was $87.00 with a 20% re-service rate. One of the largest expenses that can bankrupt a company is re-services. The problem is most companies don't track it. My advice to you is please keep track of this stat it could bankrupt your company. A re-service rate of 10% should be acceptable.

Now let me tell you what happened when I started packaging my services. Packaging my services was the first thing that happened that set me apart from all my competitors. The second thing I noticed is my customers actually wanted services done in a certain way that I never knew before. The problem is we all think we know what our customers want, and we don't. You can learn a lot from your customers so pay attention to what they tell you. As you develop your packages you'll learn what they want.

My average ticket after packaging my services went from an average of $87.00 a ticket to $222.00 a ticket but the most important thing is my re-services went down to 5%. It doesn't take a genius to see I was making a lot more money.

The trick I learned in packaging is to have a really expensive one like the platinum the ultimate whatever you want to call it. You'll be surprised how many people will buy it. Our most expensive package was called "The stay clean package". We sold about one a month and the average ticket was $2,000.00 for a carpet cleaning job. I never thought in a million years people would pay that kind of money to have their carpets cleaned but they did.

The next two packages we had were called "Value Package" and the "Budget Package". As you go through the packages I've inserted in this book you'll see that they are priced basically the same. We sold about 15 value packages a month and over 100 budget packages a month. My goal was always to make at least $100.00 an hour. After tracking all these packages my average was about $125.00 an hour for the value and the budget. The stay cleaned average was $175.00 to $200.00 an hour.

Another important thing you should know is after I started packaging my customers changed. I started doing work for the type of customers I was looking for. My perfect customers are middle-class people who will pay a fair price for services done. Some people say you should go with the really rich. I have done work for the really rich and one thing I found is you will work for every penny. I always made the most money and I mean profit with the middle-class.

I want you to know which ever packages our customers choose they always got their money's worth.

Let's get started with packaging your services. The first thing I want you to do to is go on the Internet and look at some of your competitor's websites. See how many, if any, are packaging their services. Don't believe all this mumbo-jumbo that you don't have any competitors because you do, every business does. Any business that you can make money at will have competitors that's just a fact of life. When I talk about packages I am talking about packages that the customer can understand not all this technical jargon that people could care less about.

The two things I want you to look for are how many packages they offer, if you can find one at all. First rule, there should never be more than 3 packages. If you have more than 3 packages it just confuses your customers and prospects. The second thing I want you to look for is how the packages are written. The problem with most business owners is they get too technical.

Let me give you one quick example: I told you my background is carpet cleaning. The problem with most carpet cleaners is they want to tell their customers all about the technical stuff and the expensive equipment they have. Let me tell you a little secret unless you have invented a special machine that no one else can buy, then anyone can buy the equipment you have. Your equipment is not going to set you apart from your competitors it's your service and that's one thing money can't buy. Most customers don't care about your equipment. There is always an exception to any rule. Sometimes you may have to work with an engineer; they may want more technical information.

I found that most people only care about these four things.

1. How much will it cost?
2. When can you do it?
3. How long will it take?
4. Do you guarantee your services?

You'll find that these are the basic questions you will receive from most customers in almost any service business. Let me show you the packages I had put together for my carpet cleaning business. Remember what I said I can help you with your packages. Just email me at Bob@marketingforservicebusiness.com I will just need to know a little bit about your business.

These packages are for carpet cleaning.

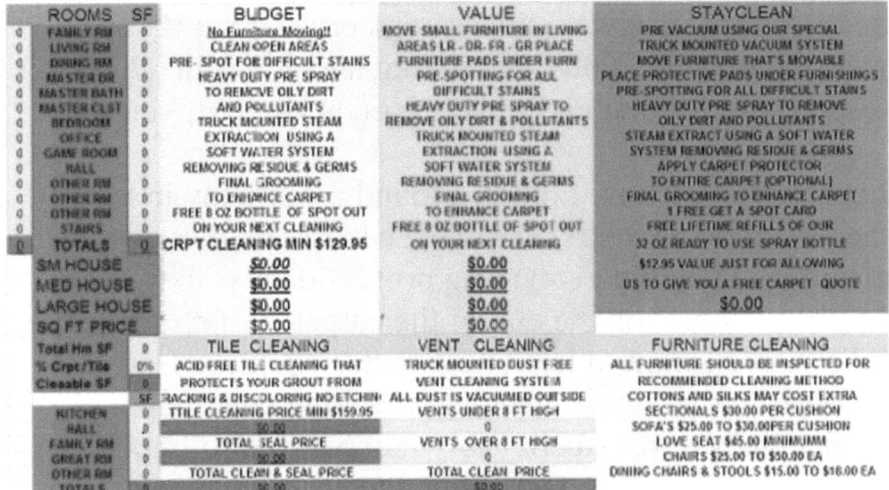

I made a lot of money with these packages!!

Remember what I said: keep your packages simple

When you design your own packages make sure their designed to be as profitable as possible. There are always other services you can offer. My rule of thumb for this is if I can't make money at it I don't do it. I would just sub it out to someone that wanted to do it plus I would make a commission and they would give me referrals.

Let me give you one example. Some of my competitors were building oriental carpet cleaning pits. First thing you had to do is get trained, that cost you time and money.

Then you had to buy all the equipment that cost you more money. Then after the training you really weren't trained because there is always a learning curve. What if you're working on a $45,000 Oriental rug and you ruin it? Who is responsible for that nightmare? You guessed it, you are.

Let me tell you how I did it. I found a company in town that had over 35 years' experience in Oriental carpet cleaning. They did everything professionally, they even fixed the tassels on the end of the carpets. That's something I didn't even want to learn how to do. Their process involved professional cleaning, mending and wrapping. Their prices were unbelievably inexpensive so I could mark up my price by 100% and make a great profit at no risk to me. All my competitors with giant egos lost money and ruined carpets with their cleaning pits.

Don't let your ego run your business; your common sense will win every time. Don't let some salesperson sell you on something that involves a lot of money. Ask yourself: how is this salesperson is making their money? On their program or on selling you their program.

I'm not asking you to buy anything extra. Just use what you have and I know you can make this work. Please just keep it simple.

The packages you saw are not technical at all. They're designed for the costumer to understand exactly what to expect from our company. Everything is written in plain English; don't get technical unless they ask you to. Following this simple rule you'll make more money and have less re-services. I will show you how to basically eliminate re-services in the following chapters.

I did my packages in an Excel spreadsheet. The reason I did it that way is because you can change the formulas if you want to change your prices. Another reason why I did it that way is because some customer may ask you how you got these prices.
If that situation comes up all you have to say is: I don't know it's in a computer program. Remember we are in this computer crazy age and most people think that computers are pretty smart. I found that most prospects will accept that answer. Remember what I said, keep it simple.

3. Your Phone Is Your Life Line

You're Phone

Your phone is your life so let's start with how to answer your phone properly.

Most companies answer their phone this way:

Thank you for calling ABC services, how may I help you? Really!

You want to give everyone that calls your company a wow affect. The wow affect makes them feel important and in turn you will get their full attention.

Use this script:

Thank you for choosing ABC services, my name is _____ who do I have the pleasure of speaking with today?

You're Phone Message

As you know the world is changing faster than ever before, the one thing that never changes no matter what is great customer service. In this world of technology more and more customers just accept the fact that they will be left on hold so that is where multi-tasking came from, bad service. Everyone has gone to a phone tree instead of someone live. I hope you haven't.

The phone message is where you are training your customers what to expect from your company. They should expect the unexpected from you and your company.

Many companies have phone scripts that goes like this: Hello, thank you for calling ABC services we can't take your call, leave your name and number and we will get back to you. Does that's make them feel important? I don't think so. When you use that script you will be just like all the other companies.

Use this voice message, it really works:

> Hello and thank you for choosing ABC services as your (mention your service) professional. We value you as a customer. We are currently servicing another important customer like you, so please leave your name and contact information and we will return your call as soon as we can. Thank you again for being a loyal customer of ABC services.

Do you see what is implied in the voice message?

You are showing all your customers that you care about them. Secondly, you are showing all your potential customers how you treat your existing customers. It's a win, win!

3.1. How to Sell Your Packages

How to Sell Your Packages

Like I said you want to give all your prospects and customers the wow affect every time they call. Always make everyone that calls your company think they're special

Use this script:

> Thank you for choosing ABC services, my name is _____ who do I have the pleasure of speaking with today?

This script is designed to give you enough time to find a customer in your database if you are using a computer. The truth of the matter is people that call your company the most you will probably remember anyway. Now that you know who you are speaking to half the battle is already won.

When you are speaking to a current customer after you've implemented my system it's easy to schedule an appointment; most repeat customers want the same service they has the last time. Some customers will add on some extra services.

Whenever a prospect calls your office you should be interviewing them. These are the questions that I have found to be most successful.

Questions for prospects:

1. How did you hear about our company? (Referral program)
2. How can I help you today?
3. When was the last time you had your (in my business, carpets clean).

Just a side note if you are an AC person, plumber or garage repair company they are probably calling because something is broken. The next question should be: **who repaired your item the last time?** If they don't remember then that's one thing. If they do remember asked them why they're not using that company. Then you'll know what went wrong. Sometimes people will complain that your prices are too high. Then you can ask them why they're not using the last company they had. If they say they went out of business that you can explain to them why you charge what you do.

Now that you know what services they need you have a starting point.

One of the biggest mistakes service companies make, is they don't explain in plain English what their services are, in other words what are their customers paying for. When you see a service for $100 and another one for $80 and you don't know what the differences is, which service would you pick> I think the answer is obvious; that's why I stopped doing coupons.

If it is just a service call this is where you get a chance to sell your packages.

Remember always start with your most expensive package. It is a lot easier to go down in price than to go up in price. As you can see by my packages I have one extremely expensive and too price right next to each other.

Now that you have the appointment set in a basic price you can tell them about the no-nonsense guarantee. We will go through that in the next chapter.

4. No Nonsense Guarantee

The No Nonsense Guarantee

Guaranteeing your services is where I see companies make their biggest mistake.

For Example:

"We have a 100% guarantee." What makes you different from all the other companies?

"We have on time guarantee". Why would any company do that? What if a customer wants more work done are you going walk away from that money. That's the most profitable money you can make.

"We have a 100% money back guarantee". Are you serious? This opens the door for dishonest customers to rip you off. Don't do it! I am speaking from experience.

Other companies print up some ridiculous certificate. That certificate ends up in the trash after you leave. Customers see it as a worthless piece of paper. You have to print and pay for that paper; it is a waste of your time and money. Don't worry if they are not happy, you'll be the 1st to know.

What I am about to show you is not only the best guarantee there is but it sets you up for a marketing strategy that very few companies are using. It's simple and won't cost you a dime.

Please use this guarantee script word for word, do not change it.

Use this script after you have scheduled the appointment unless the customer ask you first, it works just as well either way.

> [Mrs. \ Mr.] <u>Customer</u>, have you heard about our no-nonsense guarantee? We call back each and every customer that we service the next business day. If for any reason you are not satisfied with our service we will come back and make it right.

> When is the best time to call you tomorrow?

That's it, it's just that simple. You have just received permission to call your customer back; how sweet is that?

Now you can set up the next appointment when you call back. You also have a chance to explain your referral system. This simple callback will accomplish three things.

1. You will make sure your customers are happy.
2. You have an opportunity to schedule the next appointment.
3. You also have the opportunity to get referrals

Remember how I said everything comes in threes.

5. The Money Maker Follow-Up Call

The Follow-Up Call

As you know everything is about timing and that is especially true when it comes to the follow-up call. This is where companies make their biggest and most expensive mistake.

For the best results, your follow-up call should be made within 24 hours of the service. The longer you wait the less chance you have of making this a success. The reason is the longer you wait the more the wow affect will diminish.

The customer knows you are calling them; they gave you permission to do so when you schedule the appointment.

This is the simple script, please use it verbatim:

> Hello (Mrs.\Mr.) Customer, we were at your home on (the day not the date) doing your (services). This is (your name) with ABC services. I was calling to see if everything looks A LITTLE BETTER.

If you are a repair service company you can say working a little better. (The reason you say a little better is you want your customer to tell you how much better it is). Also ask "if the technician was kind, courteous and polite while he/she was at your home?" It's more personal if you use the technician's name.

This is where it gets good:

This is where you get the opportunity to schedule the next appointment.

Note: Whatever service business you're in use an expert other than yourself to tell them when they should schedule their next service.

For example: If you are a AC company tell them the AC manufacturer recommends we should come out and service your AC in 6 months. Always make someone else the expert. By making someone else the expert it will show your customers that you are learning from a professional other than yourself.

When I used this system we pre-schedule about 75% of all our customers for their next appointment. This is great repeat business and it did not cost you a dime. For us not only did it keep our trucks busy but we handle any complaints as they happened. Even if you have reschedules and you will, you won't be losing your customers to your competition. **Sweet!!**

Referrals:

(Mrs.\ Mr.) Customer before I forget I want to tell you how you can get qualify for free movie tickets. Whenever someone calls our company we always ask them how they heard about us. When you refer us to your family and friends please tell them to mention your name and we will send you free movie tickets. Can you think of a friend, neighbor or family member that we can call? I would be happy to take that information right now.

Note: This is another mistake companies make after you asked that question, make sure you wait for the answer your customer is thinking. If they say "no" than use the script below.

(Mrs.\ Mr.) <u>Customer</u> when you do think of someone the best way to make sure you receive the movie tickets is to call us with their information and we will handle it from there. When we call you back **after the work has been completed** to give you your movie tickets we will tell you how the service went. We want you to be confident your referrals are receiving the same level of service that you did. 90% of our new business comes thru referrals from satisfied customers like you.

Thanks again for using ABC services and we will see you on the _____ have a great day.

When you call someone and there is no one home use this script:

Hello (Mrs.\Mr.) <u>Customer,</u> we were at your home on (the day not the date) doing your (services). This is (your name) with ABC services. I was calling to see if everything looks A LITTLE BETTER. Also ask if the technician was kind courteous and polite while he was at your home. It's more personal if you use the technician's name. Thank you again for using ABC services for your Services. Please call me at your earliest convenience at 555 – 555 – 5555.

Oh! I almost forgot to mention you qualify for our price guarantee program. Please call me so I can go over the details with you. I also want to tell you how you can receive movie tickets just for giving us a referral. Thanks again for choosing ABC services for your service needs. Again I can be reached at 555-555 – 5555 Monday through Friday 830 to 5 PM.

In the case were they don't call you back use this script.

Hello (Mrs.\Mr.) Customer I called you yesterday and left you a message. I want you to know our company prides ourselves on making sure all of our customers are totally satisfied. If you could please call me your name at your earliest convenience. My number is 555 – 555 – 5555. I'm here Monday through Friday from 830 to 5 looking forward to hearing from you.

When you call me back please asked how you can take advantage of our price guarantee program. I also want to tell you how you can receive movie tickets just for giving us a referral. Thanks again for choosing ABC services for your service needs. If you could please call me <u>your name</u> at your earliest convenience. My number is 555 – 555 – 5555. I'm here Monday through Friday from 830 to 5 looking forward to hearing from you.

6. Bonus Chapter Referrals

Bonus Chapter Referrals

Let's talk about referrals.

Most marketing gurus will tell you that they get referrals from their customers every time they ask but you know that's not true. After you have any service done do you have a referral? I know I don't. The truth is that most people can't think of anyone to refer you to when you call them back. Why? Because they are not prepared.

As I mentioned before you will pre-schedule about 75% of your customers with the follow-up call. So what do you do for the rest of your customers? You send them a postcard that has a discount towards the next service.

Make the postcard itself be the discount, in other words they must use the postcard itself to receive the discount. They can give it to a friend if they choose.

You will save money because you don't have to insert a coupon that will get lost. The postcard itself is the discount.

Also everyone that sees that post-card will see your company's name and the discount.

7. Last Words

Last Words

I know these strategies work. I used these strategies for over 30 years in 3 states. By the way, all the customers we called always thanked us for the follow-up call. Do you know why? Because no one is doing it! Just think about all the money you have lost by not following up with your customers.

After all the work, money and time spent developing a new customer relationship, by not doing a simple follow-up call some other company could be servicing them right now. Most likely they are, of course how would you know you haven't spoken to them since you last service them?

The follow-up call stops customers from going to your competition. If you have any customers that are not happy the follow-up call will get that problem solved.

My last word of advice is nothing happens until you make it happen, so take action today.

If you want help please email me at
Bob@marketingforservicebusiness.com

I have 3 different programs to choose from **imagine that**.

Thanks again,
Bob Brunelle Arizona USA

8. About The Author

Bob as he likes to be called has owned 4 different business that he started from scratch and sold for a substantial profit. None of the business he started had any cash reserves. Bob's first business was started with $20 in his pocket and $20 in his wife pocket. Bob and his wife took 3 loans to get the loan to buy his 1st business.

Bob has been married for 41 years has one daughter who is currently in the insurance industry. Bob says without my loving and understanding wife I could not have achieved the level of business success. Bob now semi-retired his passion is to help others business owners with their business. Bob says what made me the business man I am today is over 30 years of trial and error.

Bob believes that in today's fast paced world great customer service is needed more than ever before. Customers have just accepted that great customer service is gone.

Two things Bob preaches to business owners time and time again:

1. Know your numbers run a profit and loss statement monthly.
2. Build your business from the inside with great customer service.

Bob is available on a for consulting please email at Bob@marketingforservicebusiness.com

Notes

Notes

www.ingramcontent.com/pod-product-compliance
Lightning Source LLC
Chambersburg PA
CBHW021449170526
45164CB00001B/451